INDIGENOUS AMERICAN CULTURES

Celebrating the CHUMASH

ANNE ACCARDI

Mitchell Lane
PUBLISHERS

Parent and Caregiver Tips for Creating Nonfiction Readers

The high-interest topics in the ***Indigenous American Cultures*** series are sure to get your young reader excited about reading nonfiction. While exploring a fascinating subject, your reader will be introduced to new facts, ideas, and vocabulary.

Tips for Reading Nonfiction

Talk about Nonfiction

Explain that nonfiction books provide facts about real-world topics. When readers read nonfiction, they gain a rich understanding of the world. They build background knowledge that provides a foundation for learning and academic success.

Look at the Parts

This book contains the following helpful features. Share the purpose of each feature with your reader.

Photos, Captions, and Graphic Aids

The photos, captions, maps, diagrams, time lines, and other graphic aids in nonfiction texts contain a wealth of information. Help your reader identify different ways information can be displayed.

Sidebars

These extra tidbits of information help satisfy readers' curiosity and expand their knowledge.

Table of Contents

Located at the front of the book, this list shows the big ideas within the text and the page numbers where they can be found.

Glossary

Located at the back of the book, the glossary defines key words and phrases that are related to the topic. These words and phrases can be found in the text in colored type.

Comprehension Questions (Fact Check)

Multiple-choice questions help readers self-check to make sure they understand what they read.

Index

Located at the back of the book, the index is an alphabetical list of topics and the page numbers where they can be found.

With a little help and guidance, your reader will be on their way to enjoying and learning from nonfiction books.

Mitchell Lane
PUBLISHERS

mitchelllanepub.com

2001 SW 31st Avenue
Hallandale, FL 33009

First Edition, 2026.
Author: Anne Accardi
Designer: Rhea Magaro
Editor: Kim Thompson

Series: Indigenous American Cultures
Title: Celebrating the Chumash / by Anne Accardi

Hallandale, FL : Mitchell Lane Publishers, [2026]

Library bound ISBN: 979-8-89260-553-3
Paperback ISBN: 979-8-89260-589-2
eBook ISBN: 979-8-89260-560-1

PHOTO CREDITS
Alamy: Sandyman, cover, 1; Debra Behr cover, 1; ZUMA Press, Inc, cover, 1; UtCon Collection, 7; Nature and Science, 8; North Wind Picture Archives 9; Leigh Green, 12; Danita Delimont, 17; Chuck Place, 17; ClassicStock, 20; Dorling Kindersley ltd, 22; Eyal Nahmias, 28, 29; iStock: Nature, food, landscape, travel cover, 1; Public Domain: NPR, 5; Mark Mauno 6; Wiki, 12, 14, 15, 16, 27; NPS, 23; 2017 Secretaría de Cultura CDMX 26; Shutterstock: Weredragon, 4; MarioBrother2024, 5; CSNafzger 10; Bram Reusen 11; HannaTor 13; Gummy Bear 18; Pixel-Shot 18; ShutterstockProfessional, 18; Nick Pecker, 19; Viacheslav Nikolaenko, 21; HannaTor, 24, 25; Ovidiu Hrubaru, 29;

CONTENTS

A CHUMASH CONNECTION

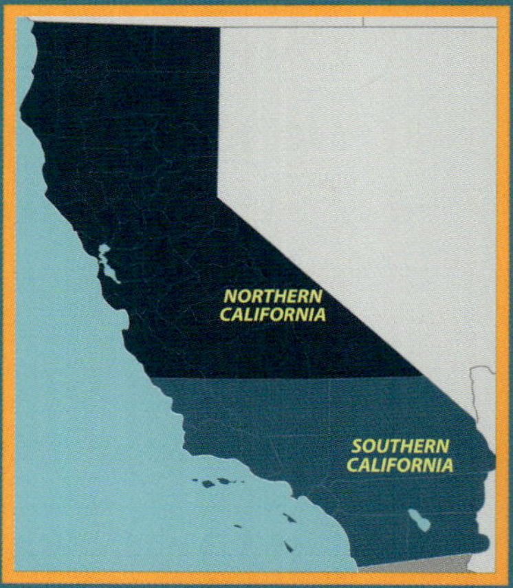

Have you ever walked along a beach, searching for seashells? If so, you were following in the footsteps of the **Indigenous** Chumash people. The name *Chumash* means "shell bead money maker." Long ago, the Chumash carved shells to make a form of **currency** called *'alchum*. They used it to trade with other tribes.

The Chumash are one of the oldest tribes in North America. For over 13,000 years, they have lived along the Pacific Ocean on land that is now Southern California.

Culture Close-Up

Chumash shell beads may have been the first form of money used in the Americas.

CHUMASH HISTORY

In ancient times, the Chumash lived in hundreds of villages. Many were near the ocean. The villages stretched most of the way from modern-day Los Angeles to San Francisco, California. Some were on the Channel Islands.

This model shows what a Chumash village may have looked like long ago.

The Chumash population grew to more than 20,000. Some villages grew into towns. The people were rich in natural resources. They built canoes. They hunted and fished. They traded with people as far away as present-day Nevada and Arizona.

This Chumash man was photographed in the late 1800s.

Culture Close-Up

Each Chumash village had family homes, workshops, sports fields, an area for dancing, and a place for religious rituals.

In the 1700s, Spanish explorers came. They brought diseases that killed Chumash people. They set up **missions** and forced the Chumash to live and work there. Some Chumash fought back, but soldiers burned their homes.

For a time, it was legal in California to enslave and kill Indigenous people. By 1910, there were few Chumash left. But the Chumash survived. Today, there are more than 10,000 people with Chumash **ancestry** in the United States. Many live on the Santa Ynez **Reservation** in California.

EXPLORING CHUMASH PLACES

To learn more about the Chumash, you can visit Santa Cruz Island. The Chumash call it Limuw. The large Chumash village Swaxil once stood on its shores.

Trails let visitors explore the beauty of Chumash homelands. You can see island oak and ironwood trees. They gave the people acorns for eating and wood for building. You can see the rocky cliffs where the Chumash mined **chert** to make tools for carving shell beads.

Culture Close-Up

Golden poppies grow on Santa Cruz Island. There are so many that you can see their bright color from the mainland. The flowers appear in Chumash stories. The Chumash used them to make tea and medicine.

You can also visit the Chumash Indian Museum in Thousand Oaks, California. You can tour a recreated village. It has traditional dome-shaped homes called *'aps*. A cave exhibit shows how the Chumash used painting and carving tools to make **petroglyphs**.

Visitors can learn about **native** plants that the Chumash used for food and medicine. The yucca plant was used to make baskets and fishing lines.

The leaves and roots of the yucca plant can be eaten and used to make rope, sandals, shampoo, and other useful things.

Culture Close-Up

An old oak tree in the Santa Lucia Mountains shows ancient carvings. For a long time, no one knew who carved these arborglyphs. Now, historians think they were made by the Chumash.

CHUMASH LANGUAGES

Seven different languages were spoken in Chumash villages. Today, very few people know how to speak them.

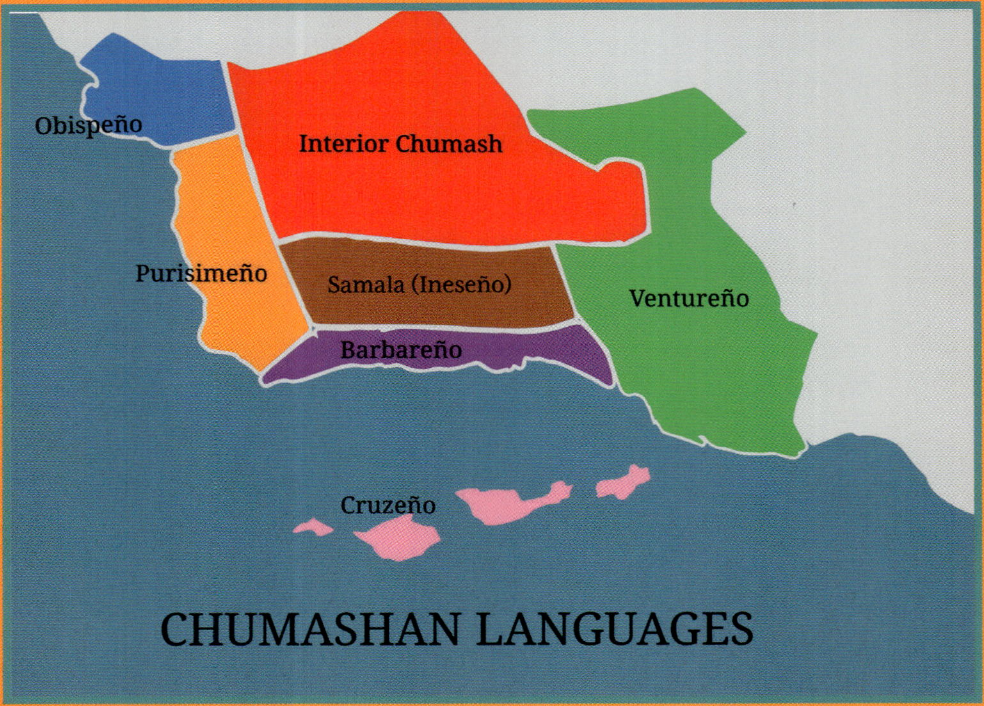

In 2008, the Santa Ynez Band of Chumash started a language program. It helps people learn their language, which is called Samala. They made a dictionary and other teaching materials. Now, young people can speak the language and help keep Chumash culture alive.

Culture Close-Up

Practice these Samala words and phrases.

Haku. (Hello.)

Tikali'? (How are you?)

Ka sč^{h}olit. (I'm doing well.)

Ma ktɨ ka (My name is)

Kiwana'n. (Goodbye.)

HONORING CHUMASH TRADITIONS

Beautiful Chumash baskets have complex designs. They are admired around the world. Once, the Chumash made special baskets for storing food, holding water, and fishing. They were woven from dried plants such as rush and sumac.

Today, Chumash artists continue the tradition. They work to protect the land where native plants grow. The Santa Ynez Band of Chumash gives classes in basket weaving.

Culture Close-Up

Chumash artists create beautiful objects using natural materials such as shells and native plants.

Long ago, the Chumash were experts at making medicine from plants. They mixed bark, roots, and flowers with minerals and sea water. Poison oak was used to treat skin diseases. Chia seeds helped eye problems. People wore chuchupate root to protect them from rattlesnakes.

Some Chumash people still practice traditional medicine. They try to preserve the close relationship their ancestors had with native plants.

The datura plant can be poisonous or even fatal. But the ancient Chumash used it during religious ceremonies and for treating severe wounds.

Culture Close-Up

Some remedies were unusual. To treat diarrhea, the Chumash swallowed live ants!

Games have always been important to the Chumash. One favorite game is shinny. It is like field hockey. Players use sticks to hit a small wooden ball into the other team's goal. In the past, entire Chumash villages played against each other during ceremonies.

Today, the Native American Shinny League (NASL) continues the tradition. It teaches the game to kids ages 12 and up.

Chumash people have played shinny for generations.

Culture Close-Up

Ancient Chumash people made stick-bows from natural materials. Using them for archery was a good way to practice hunting skills. People on the Santa Ynez Reservation still make and use stick-bows today.

CHUMASH CELEBRATIONS

Long ago, the Chumash made plank canoes, or tomols. Tomols traveled up and down the coast for trading. They could carry 10 people and hundreds of pounds of fish and other goods.

Today, Chumash people hold a yearly Tomol Channel Crossing. They paddle a tomol for 23 miles (37 kilometers) across the Santa Barbara Channel. When they arrive, there is a celebration with singing and dancing.

Culture Close-Up

Tomols are the oldest ocean-going ships in North America. They were built with logs held together by yop. Yop is a glue made from asphaltum, a sticky substance found in the ocean after oil seeps up from underground.

Each year, the Santa Ynez Band of Chumash holds an Inter-Tribal **Powwow**. Indigenous dancers and drummers from all over North America come to compete for thousands of dollars in prize money.

Visitors enjoy traditional foods. Indigenous artists display their work. The powwow is a special way for the Chumash to share their culture with others.

FAMOUS FACES

Many well-known people have Chumash ancestry. Lorna Dee Cervantes is an award-winning writer. Her family is Chumash and Mexican. She writes poems about justice, **heritage**, and other important themes.

Lorna Dee Cervantes

John Olguin was the director of the Cabrillo Marine Museum in Los Angeles. He loved the ocean and spent his life teaching others about it. In the 1970s, he organized some of the first whale-watching trips in California.

John Olguin

Culture Close-Up

Maria Solares was one of the last fluent speakers of the Chumash language Samala. Language expert John P. Harrington listened to her stories and took careful notes. This helped preserve the language for future generations.

LESSONS FROM THE CHUMASH

Ancient Chumash people had a close relationship to the ocean. They understood how to use the land responsibly. They showed respect for natural resources.

Chumash people celebrate their culture and honor their heritage. Their stories and traditions can teach all Americans important lessons about living in harmony with nature.

GLOSSARY

ancestry (AN-ces-tree): belonging to a line of family members who came before you; your ancestors

chert (churt): a hard, sharp rock similar to flint

currency (KUR-uhn-see): the form of money used by a nation or a people

heritage (HER-i-tij): traditions and beliefs that people consider to be an important part of their history

Indigenous (in-DI-juh-nuhs): the earliest known inhabitants of a place

missions (MISH-uhnz): churches or other places where missionaries live as they try to spread their faith to others

native (NAY-tiv): living or growing naturally in a certain place

petroglyphs (PE-truh-glifs): ancient carvings or paintings on rock, often on cave walls

powwow (POU-wou): a gathering of Indigenous Americans that is organized for social or ceremonial reasons and that may include traditional singing, dancing, and drumming

reservation (rez-ur-VAY-shuhn): an area of land set aside by the government for ownership by an Indigenous American tribe

FACT CHECK

1. The land where the ancient Chumash lived is now the state of ________.

   A. South Dakota B. Washington C. California

2. Samala is a ________.

   A. language B. tree C. basket-weaving method

3. What is a tomol?

   A. a food B. a game C. a canoe

4. The Chumash are experts at ___________.

   A. farming B. horseback riding C. using native plants

Answers: 1. C, 2. A, 3. C, 4. C

FURTHER READING

Jennings, Dorothy. *The Chumash*. Rosen Publishing Group, 2017.

Miller, Joe E. *Cave of the Birdman: A Chumash Adventure Story*. Lizard's Mouth Press, 2022.

Weso, Tom Pecore. *Native American Stories for Kids: 12 Traditional Stories from Indigenous Tribes across North America*. Callisto Kids, 2022.

ON THE INTERNET

Chumash Indian Museum
www.chumashmuseum.org/educational-resources
Find videos and other resources about Chumash history and culture.

National Park Service: Channel Islands
www.nps.gov/chis/planyourvisit/channel-islands-live-nps.htm
Watch live broadcasts from the islands, including webcams on bald eagles and other animals.

Native American Hall of Fame
nativehalloffame.org
Find biographies of well-known Indigenous Americans from the 1860s to the present.

INDEX

ABOUT THE AUTHOR

Anne Accardi is an author from Kansas City, Missouri. She is thrilled to share facts about Indigenous Americans with young people. She loves history and finding ways to connect the past with the present and future. When she's not reading or writing, you can find Anne in a library, museum, or movie theater.